CONTENTS

THE ERECHTHEION

These magnificent caryatid statues, overlooking Athens, are part of the Erechtheion temple on the Acropolis. Built over 2,400 years ago, they are an impressive reminder of the ancient Greeks and their culture.

LIFE IN ANCIENT GREECE

BY

JOHN GUY

WHO WERE THE ANCIENT GREEKS?

Ancient Greece is said to be the 'cradle of civilization' in Europe, meaning where civilized society began. Unlike Rome and other civilizations that followed, it was not one centrally controlled empire. Early Greek civilizations were influenced by Egypt and Sumeria. The first was the Minoan, based on the island of Crete, which lasted from c.2000 BCE to 1400 BCE. On the mainland, the main civilization was the Mycenaean, c.1600-1100 BCE. Then Greece entered a 'Dark Age', and very little is known about it. In the 8th century BCE, a number of city-states emerged. They all had links with each other, and each rose to power through war, rather than by agreement.

PULLING TOGETHER

Although the Greek city-states acted independently, one of the few times they worked together was in the Trojan Wars c.1184 BCE. The Mycenaean king, Agamemnon, united the Greeks against Troy, defeating them with the use of a huge wooden horse.

GREEK TOWNS

Greek towns were built on hills for defence. Public and religious buildings were close together.

THE TEMPLE

The main temple was usually on the highest point of the acropolis and was meant to impress both the people and the gods.

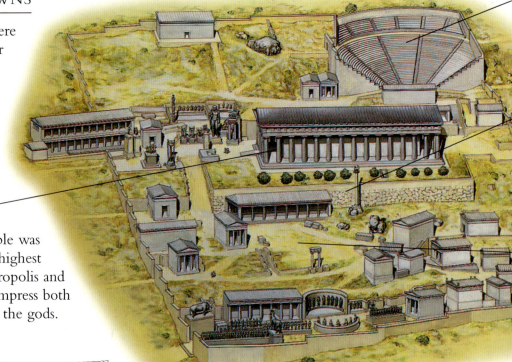

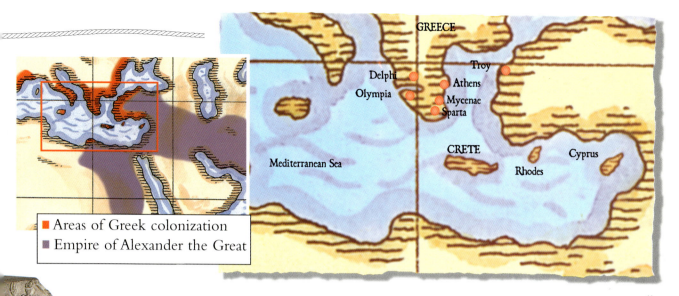

Areas of Greek colonization
Empire of Alexander the Great

GREECE
Troy
Delphi
Athens
Olympia
Mycenae
Sparta
CRETE
Mediterranean Sea
Rhodes
Cyprus

SPIRITUAL CENTRE

The Omphalos Stone
(shown here) was
thought to mark the
centre of the universe.
Zeus wanted to measure
the world, so he set two
eagles free from opposite
ends of the Earth. They
met over Delphi, so
Zeus decreed that this
was the world's centre.

THE FIRST EUROPEANS

The earliest known
civilization in Europe
was on Crete in the
eastern Mediterranean.
It was named Minoan,
after the legendary
King Minos who was
said to rule the Aegean Sea. Excavations of the
palace of Knossos in northern Crete have shown
that its people enjoyed a sophisticated lifestyle.

THE AMPHITHEATRE

Every major town had an
open-air theatre, called an
amphitheatre.

THE ACROPOLIS

At the highest
point of the town
was a citadel, or
walled enclosure.
This housed the
most important town
buildings, the temples and
government buildings.

THE AGORA

In the centre was the agora, a
large open space where
people met and
carried out business

THE COLOSSUS OF RHODES

Once part of
Macedonia,
in around 408 BCE
the islanders of
Rhodes formed
themselves into an
independent state.
The island was
unsuccessfully
besieged by Demetrios in
305-304 BCE. To mark
their victory, they built
the Colossus, a gigantic
statue of the sun god,
Helios.

FINE CRAFTSMANSHIP

As food was easily available at the town's market, not everyone needed to grow their own. Workers could develop other skills to trade and the Greek potters became fine craftsmen. Using local clay, they produced beautifully decorated items including plates, dishes, wine goblets, bottles and vases for both the home market and for export.

ELEGANT CLOTHES

This carved relief from a temple shows the typical clothes worn by wealthier Greeks. The poor wore linen or woollen clothes, but the rich could afford to buy exotic imported materials, such as fine cotton and silk from India and the East. The rich employed tailors or bought ready-made clothes from merchants.

SLAVE TRADE

Like most ancient civilizations, Greece depended on slave labour. People involved in the slave trade made a lot of money by selling slaves to wealthy Greeks to be used as cheap labour.

LIFE FOR THE RICH

The rich usually lived in large town houses, close to all the town's facilities. The very rich might have had a house in the country. Although Greek civic (public) buildings were very grand, homes were not – the rich just had larger houses than the poor. Most wealthy men worked in government or trade, so they needed to live in towns. The wives of these wealthy men lived dull lives, as their slaves did all the work.

SIMPLE TASTES

Houses, even for the rich, were basic, made from dried mud bricks (painted white to reflect the heat of the sun) or stone. They had tiled roofs, stone floors and a small open courtyard. Windows were few, to keep the inside cool and shady. The rooms were simple but comfortably furnished.

DEATH MASK

This beautiful mask of beaten gold was believed to be the funerary mask of Agamemnon, the legendary king of Mycenae. He died in the 12th century BCE. These masks were used in royal burials and show the wealth of the civilization.

RAISE YOUR GLASS

The technique of glass-blowing was not perfected until Roman times. Before that, glass was expensive and difficult to work with. Therefore, most drinking vessels were made of clay, but the rich would buy goblets made of glass to show their wealth and impress their friends.

LIFE FOR THE POOR

Although most of the remains from ancient Greece are grand, both in size and design, this does not give a correct picture of Greek society. There were some wealthy people who enjoyed a very luxurious lifestyle but most Greeks were poor, and struggled to earn a living from the land. The soil in Greece is not fertile, and the climate is very dry. This made it hard for ordinary people to have good harvests. Sometimes they had to leave their villages and move to new colonies in the empire. Otherwise, they would have starved.

EARTHENWARE

Pottery for the poorer classes was simple and practical, and rarely decorated. Life was a struggle for survival, and there was little time or money to spend on luxuries. Plates, pots and drinking vessels were usually made from unglazed clay, moulded by hand and left to dry in the sun.

BEASTS OF BURDEN

The most common beast of burden was the donkey or mule. They are very sure-footed animals, which was particularly important in the mountainous and rocky terrain of Greece. Peasant farmers often used their donkeys to travel long distances from villages to reach their fields. For the very poor, who could not afford an ox, donkeys were even used to pull the plough.

AGRICULTURE

The Greeks did not have a centrally organized system of agriculture. Each farmer grew his own food and had his own oxen to pull the plough. Poorer communities would sometimes share a team of oxen, with each family taking its turn. In order to help feed the growing population, it was necessary for the Greeks to expand their empire. They set up colonies around the Mediterranean to import any food needed.

HUMBLE HOMES

For the poor, houses were simple. They were built from dried mud bricks, plastered with wet mud and painted white to reflect the summer heat. Roofs were either thatched or tiled. The construction and style was not hugely different from houses and churches still seen in Greece today. They would have had only one main room where the whole family lived and ate.

SUBSISTENCE FARMING

Most of the population lived in remote villages, scattered throughout the land and often separated from one another by the mountains. Peasants struggled on their farms, each growing just enough to feed their own family. Luckily, most communities were close to the sea, so the poor could add fresh seafood to their diet. Any extra food was taken to market to trade for other items, such as shoes and wine. Most families would also keep a few goats for milk and cheese, and chickens for eggs.

LEISURE TIME

One of the most popular pastimes in ancient Greece was attending plays, pageants or festivals at the town's amphitheatre. Performances were free or cheap, sponsored by rich men or politicians who wanted to be popular with the people, so even the poor could enjoy the festivities. Women did not usually attend, though they were probably not actually banned from doing so.

SEAFOOD

The Mediterranean has lots of seafood, especially octopus and squid, which is still important in Greek cookery today. The usual method of cooking was to cut the tentacles into small slices and to boil or fry them in olive oil. Common fish still caught in Greek waters are tuna, mullet and mackerel.

ARBRES FRUITIERS.

Récolte des olives.

VÉRITABLE EXTRAIT DE VIANDE LIEBIG.

OLIVE GROVES

It is said that the goddess Athena introduced the olive tree to Greece. Olives were either eaten or pressed to make oil, used in cooking, rubbed into the skin, or burned for lighting. Olive trees grow well in Greece and still provide a valuable source of income for farmers today.

VINTAGE WINE

The most common drink for Greeks of all classes was wine. Sometimes this was drunk undiluted, but usually water was added. The wine was quite thick and did not keep well and was usually strained before drinking.

HOME COOKING

This terracotta figure from Crete, made in the 6th century BCE, shows a woman stirring food in a saucepan with a ladle. She may be making stew, or perhaps porridge. Vegetables were often made into a stew and eaten with bread, but the Greeks also enjoyed salads dressed with garlic and olive oil. Cooking was often done outdoors to avoid smells.

FOOD AND DRINK

The wealthy Greeks ate very well, enjoying a wide variety of foods, while the poor had to make do with a more limited diet. However, all Greeks knew the importance of good food for their health, and they had a balanced diet consisting of protein, fibre, dairy and vegetables. Most people in rural areas grew their own food and tended their own animals. Even in towns, many households kept a goat for fresh milk and cheese and perhaps a few chickens for eggs. Meat was not widely eaten by the poor, but the rich enjoyed meat, including boar, deer and rabbit. Fortunately, the waters of the Mediterranean provided a bountiful supply of seafood.

SOURCE OF PROTEIN

As many settlements were situated near the coast, the sea provided a plentiful supply of alternative protein to meat, which the poor could not afford.

DAILY BREAD

Greeks ate a lot of bread, made with wheat or barley flour. Greek bread was quite coarse and stodgy and was baked in flat, round loaves. A great favourite at breakfast-time was to soak bread in olive oil or wine, and eat it with figs or other fruit. The decorative loaf shown here was probably made for a banquet.

MUSIC AND DANCE

Music and dancing were popular with Greeks from all classes, not only as a pastime but also at religious festivals. Musicians often accompanied plays at the theatre or performed at private banquets. Common musical instruments of the time included flutes, pan-pipes, harps and lyres.

THEATRE-GOING

Most Greek cities had an amphitheatre at their centre. This was an open-air theatre where plays or performances of stories of the gods and legendary heroes were popular. The plays were usually comedies or tragedies, and all the actors wore a mask to show their character.

LEGENDARY HEROES

One of the main pastimes in the home was storytelling. Children would gather round to hear their parents tell legendary tales of past Greek heroes, or of the gods. One story was about Theseus slaying the Minotaur, a half-bull, half-man monster, kept by the legendary King Minos in a labyrinth at Knossos, Crete.

DISCUS THROWING

Statues of discus throwers seem to have been popular, and these athletes represent the spirit of the Olympic Games more than any other. Like other events, discus throwing came out of warfare. It was used to train soldiers to throw accurately.

THE OLYMPIC GAMES

The most important sports event in ancient Greece were the Olympic Games. They were first held in 776 BCE. They were then held every four years in Olympia and were put on as a way of honouring the gods. The various city-states became very competitive in the Olympic Games.

PASTIMES

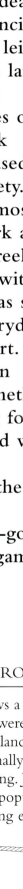

e know a great deal about how the ancient Greeks spent their leisure time because of the large amount of surviving art and artefacts, showing scenes of everyday life. Greek culture was based on a slave society. Slaves did most of the hard work and this left many Greeks, especially the rich, with free time. Leisure was seen as important in everyday life, especially sport. Sport provided an important method of training for warfare and was a way of honouring the gods. Music, dancing and theatre-going were other popular pastimes, as were board games, gambling and horse and chariot racing.

THE JAVELIN THROWER

This stone relief shows a Greek javelin thrower. Javelins were long, light spears specially balanced for throwing, and were originally made as a form of weapon training. Javelin throwing became very popular at sporting events.

FASHION

Greeks of all classes spent a great deal of time and money on their hairstyles, clothes and jewellery. The rivalry between the city-states included fashion, with people of one state thinking they were more fashionable than the others. Clothes were often white or brightly coloured. The poorer classes wore finely spun woollen clothes and the rich showed their wealth by wearing silks and cottons imported from the East. Women's clothing was often made of light materials, and male and female athletes usually competed naked.

ELABORATE HAIRSTYLES

Women used decorative pins and slides to hold their hair in place, while for men it was fashionable to curl their hair, as shown here.

NOVELTY VALUE

This beautiful perfume pot was made of decorated clay with a wax stopper. Some regions were known for producing unusual novelty ware, such as this, for export. Greeks were quite fussy about their personal hygiene, and both men and women wore perfume.

PROPER DRESS

We know a great deal about the clothes worn by ordinary men and women from the beautiful decorations on Greek pottery, such as on this vase. Clothes for men and women were quite similar; they wore simple tunics, fastened at the shoulder by a brooch.

AN AGE OF ELEGANCE

Jewellery was popular amongst all classes, and often showed a person's wealth. Poorer people wore jewellery made of cheaper materials, such as bronze or ceramics. The rich wore jewellery made of gold or silver. Although precious and semi-precious stones were used, Greek jewellers liked to use delicately crafted gold and silver pendants and chains. The replica earring shown here came from Troy (the original was dated c.2300 BCE).

REFLECTED BEAUTY

Many people might be surprised at how sophisticated Greek society was, especially amongst the upper classes. Quite a few items still in use today, which we might think of as modern, were in use in ancient Greek times. This bronze mirror has a carving of the Aphrodite, goddess of love and beauty, on its stand. The back of the panel is beautifully engraved and the front would have been highly polished to show a reflection.

SKIN DEEP

Physical exercise and caring for the body was seen as essential to good health. It was fashionable to wash regularly, not in large public baths, like the Romans, but in small tubs at home. They rubbed their bodies with olive oil to make their skin smooth. Both men and women used make-up to lighten the skin, as a sun tan was thought to be unattractive. Most people wore simple leather sandals on their feet, as worn by this girl.

ART AND ARCHITECTURE

The art and architecture of the ancient Greeks has perhaps been the most influential of any civilization. They developed a style of architecture based upon Egyptian examples. This used tall columns to support heavy lintels (horizontal pieces of stone) to create large, grand public buildings that still inspire architects today. State and religious buildings were decorated with statues and stone friezes, showing great skills in stone masonry. They were also skilful as artists, as can be seen from surviving artefacts produced at the time.

THE POTTER'S ART

Pottery can be used to date the society that created it. Greek pottery was mostly made from local clay, made on a wheel and fired in ovens. It can be roughly dated according to its design. Up to about 700 BCE, geometric patterns were popular. These were replaced by a fashion for oriental designs and black figures until around 500, BCE when the red-figure technique took over.

WALL PAINTINGS

The walls of many Greek buildings were decorated with frescoes and paintings. The wall painting shown here, with dolphins and fish, is a restoration, and comes from the Queen's Room in the Palace of Knossos, Crete (c.1500 BCE).

ARCHITECTURAL STYLES

The main features of Greek buildings were the rows of columns supporting the roof beams (lintels). The tops of the columns (capitals) were highly decorated. The three main styles were plain (known as Doric), scroll-topped (Ionic, as shown) or highly decorated with leaf and other designs (Corinthian).

THE ACROPOLIS

The acropolis was the upper fortified section of all Greek cities. This main picture shows the Acropolis in Athens, with the temple of the Parthenon at its centre, built between 447 and 432 BCE.

HEALTH AND MEDICINE

The Greeks took their interest in the study of medicine from the ancient Egyptians, whom they greatly admired. Egyptian physicians specialized in certain areas of the body and treated them alone. Greek doctors, however, looked at each part in relation to the whole body. They wanted to promote general good health and even gave a daily dose of wine to their patients. To remove infected parts, operations were sometimes carried out, but only if no other treatment had worked. Wealthy citizens lived to over the age of 70.

THE GOD OF MEDICINE

Asclepios, a son of Apollo, was the god of medicine and healing. Ancient Greeks believed that illness and disease were sent by the gods as a punishment if they were offended. In many pagan religions, the serpent (as seen here twisted round his staff) is seen as the 'life-force' flowing through all things and is held sacred.

HEALTHY LIFESTYLES

Sick people travelled many miles to look for cures at the shrines of Asclepios, where the priests prescribed herbal cures and special diets. One of the main forms of preventative medicine was exercise, to both please the gods and generate healthy well-being. Boys were encouraged to practise athletics as training for the army, and girls to prepare for healthy childbirth.

FOUNDER OF MODER MEDICINE

Hippocrates (460–377 BCE) was a famous physician. He started teaching in the open, under a plane tree (shown left). Hippocrates wrote 53 medical books, known as the Corpus. He believed that the human body was a single organism and the individual parts should not be treated separately. He established a code of medical ethics, which doctors still follow today (the Hippocratic Oath).

PERSONAL HYGIENE

The Greeks recognized the importance of personal cleanliness and hygiene to maintain good health. They did not take hot and cold plunge baths, like the Romans, but did wash frequently in private tubs in their homes. They also used olive oil to deep-cleanse the skin.

SANITATION

From a very early date, the Greeks constructed water supply and drainage systems. The two systems were kept separate to prevent the spread of disease. Good examples can be seen in the palaces and towns of Crete (c.2000 BCE), such as Malia and Knossos.

LOVE AND MARRIAGE

GODDESS OF LOVE

Aphrodite was the Greek goddess of love and beauty. On their wedding day, brides made offerings to her shrine hoping for a happy marriage.

Most marriages in ancient Greece were arranged between both sets of parents. Usually a father would select a husband (often much older) for his daughter when she reached the age of 12 or 13. When courting, a young man would pay a great deal of attention to his intended bride, but once married it was a different story. Wives were considered the property of their husbands and were expected to obey them. Married women were hardly ever allowed to meet or talk to other men unless their husband was present. In Sparta, men were not allowed to marry until the age of 20.

SPARTAN GIRLS

This statue is of a young girl from Sparta, a powerful Greek state that at one time rivalled the power of Athens. Both young men and women were encouraged to compete in athletics in order to produce a 'super race' of soldiers, and so the girls would have healthy babies. As a result of being treated more as equals, Spartan girls seemed more confident than girls from other states.

OBEDIENT WIVES

The main purpose in marriage for both a man and a woman was to give birth to sons to carry on the family line. In most of Greece, the more wealthy and important a man was, the stricter he was with his wife. She would have been confined to an area of the house called the Women's Quarter. This allowed the husband to entertain without his guests meeting his wife.

UNREQUITED LOVE

The theme of unrequited (or unreturned) love is common in Greek mythology, amongst both humans and gods. This picture shows the sun god, Apollo, and Daphne, a nymph and daughter of the river god, Peneus. Apollo fell in love with Daphne, but she did not love him. She asked the king of the gods, Zeus, for help, by praying to him. Zeus then turned Daphne into a laurel tree. This tree became sacred to Apollo, and he often wore a laurel wreath on his head in memory of his lost love.

NYMPHS

Nymphs were not gods, but also not human. They were female spirits of nature, and were always shown in art and statues as beautiful women. The Oreads were mountain nymphs and the Dryads were nymphs of wood and trees. Naiads were fresh water nymphs and the Oceanids were nymphs of salt water. Nymphs often became lovers of the gods. They could change things, too. It is said that a young, handsome man called Hylas was changed into an echo.

WOMEN AND CHILDREN

Women in Greek society were not treated very well and they had very few rights. The situation varied between the different city-states, but generally, women were looked down on. Few women were allowed to have jobs, and when they married, any money or property they had went to their husbands.

Poorer women had more freedom than the rich. They were allowed to work and could meet their friends at the market. Sons were treated well, but girls were married off as soon as possible.

GIVE UP YOUR TOYS

From the age of 12 children were treated as young adults. Boys gave up their toys to Apollo, and girls to his twin sister, Artemis to show they had grown up. Artemis was the goddess of the hunt.

HELEN OF TROY

Women were owned by men in ancient Greece. When Paris, prince of Troy, took Helen, wife of the Spartan king Menelaus, away, the Greeks were furious. They united their armies and, according to mythology, besieged Troy for ten years in order to rescue Helen.

HELD IN THE BALANCE

Greek fathers had the right to decide whether a newborn baby lived or died. If the child was sickly, or a girl, they may abandon the baby, if they could not afford to keep it. These babies were left outside to die, though some might be saved by childless families.

CHILDREN AT PLAY

A typical Greek childhood was quite short. By the age of 12, boys were doing physical training for the army, and girls might already be married. Those children who remained at home after then, were expected to help support the family. Children played with a variety of toys, including dolls, soldiers and board games. Greek families were quite large, but many children died.

LEARNING BY ROTE

At seven, boys from rich families began their education. The usual subjects were reading, writing, arithmetic, poetry and music, learnt by reciting out loud. Very rarely, the daughters of rich families received private tuition.

KOUROS

This marble statue of a naked young boy is called a 'kouros'. They were placed in shrines dedicated to Apollo, god of light and healing. It is believed that children were used in some religious rituals, to represent goodness.

A WOMAN'S LOT

A woman's place in ancient Greek society was not a happy one. As well as helping on the family farm, poorer women had to do the cooking, cleaning, spinning and weaving. If a woman did not marry, she stayed under the control of her father or brothers.

ALEXANDER THE GREAT

Alexander became king of Macedon at the age of 20. He went on to become one of the world's greatest leaders. He managed to unite all the individual city-states into one nation. He built an empire that stretched from Italy in the west to Kashmir in the east and Egypt in the south. He died in Babylon aged just 32.

STRONGHOLDS

At the centre, and usually the highest point, of every Greek town, was a fortified citadel, known as an acropolis. Strong walls and gates protected temples and important buildings.

NAVAL POWER

The Greeks relied heavily on the strength of their fleet in keeping control of the Aegean Sea. This was important because many Greek colonies were on islands. The fastest and most powerful Greek ship was the trireme.

THE TROJAN WAR

Sieges could last many years. The usual practice was to burn the crops surrounding a city and cut off all supply routes to stop food getting through. The Greek army eventually won the Trojan War by trickery. Soldiers hidden inside a huge wooden horse, supposedly left behind as a gift to the Trojans, opened the city gates at night and let in the Greek army.

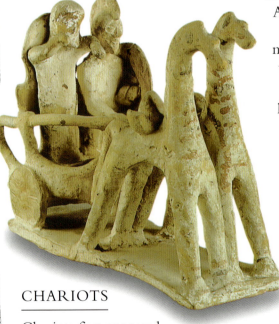

CHARIOTS

Chariots first appeared in Sumeria and Egypt around 3,000 BCE. They were small two-wheeled carts pulled by horses, and they carried two men, a driver and an armed soldier. The Greek army used them to charge the enemy lines.

WAR AND WEAPONS

*U*nlike other great civilizations, ancient Greece was never a united country. For complicated reasons, the region developed as a number of independent city-states. Although each of these mini-states was influenced by the others, they were often fiercely independent. Quarrels and wars between the individual states were common, and each seems to have taken it in turn to become the most dominant and powerful state. When war broke out, it was the duty of every male citizen to help fight if needed, as there were no permanent enemy armies, except in Sparta. Only on three occassions did the various Greek states unite to act together: during the Trojan wars, the Persian wars and under Alexander the Great.

GREEK FIRE

This vase decoration shows Odysseus, a legendary Greek hero, returning from war. Greek ships (called galleys) were quite large and often carried siege engines, such as catapults and ballistas, which could throw missiles weighing up to 25 kilos. Sometimes, burning missiles were hurled amongst enemy ships.

MILITARY SERVICE

Greece did not have a full-time army (except in Sparta). Instead, all men trained to fight from the age of 20, ready to be called up. Foot soldiers, called Hoplites, paid for their own equipment. They had a short sword, spear, bronze shield, breastplate and helmet.

CRIME AND PUNISHMENT

Ancient Greece was not a united country with one central system of government. It is difficult for us today to understand the different systems of government and law that were used in the city-states. Some states, such as Lesbos, were quite free but other states, such as Sparta, were more military, and their laws were different because of this. In Athens, the ruling classes were driven out, and a democratic system of government and law-making was introduced. Only certain classes of citizens could vote, but ordinary people could have their say about government at meetings called 'assemblies'. Not all Greek states were democracies, though. Many people did not approve of the democratic system, and Greece finally returned to a monarchy. At this time the crime rate was generally low.

BANKRUPTCY

If a farmer got into debt (which happened often when crops failed in the poor soils), his possessions could be seized, and he could be sold into slavery for bankruptcy. The Athenian politician Solon (c.640–558 BCE), shown above, introduced new laws to stop this practice.

SACRED TEMPLES

To most Greeks, religion was a part of everyday life. Damaging temples, such as this magnificent temple of Apollo in Delphi, would have been seen as a crime against the whole community. The main goal in life was to serve one's own community, and so the worst punishment for many crimes was banishment, which denied the criminal all the benefits of the Greek way of life. Murder and corruption were punishable by execution.

DEATH BY POISONING

The teachings of the philosopher Socrates were considered so shocking, that he was thought a bad influence on the young. He was eventually arrested for his views, and sentenced to death by drinking hemlock (plant poison).

OSTRACISM

Citizens in the city-state of Athens had the right to punish any politician, who they thought had behaved badly, by banishing them for ten years. Citizens would cast a vote of no-confidence by writing the person's name on a piece of pottery (as shown here), called an ostrakon. The pieces were then counted, and if there were more than 6,000, the named person was banished.

PERIKLES

Although Athens was run as a democracy, not everyone approved of this system. It was still dominated by powerful statesmen, who could force through laws of their choice. The illustration shows Perikles, who was elected 'strategos' (leader of the military) for 14 years between 443 and 429 BCE.

TRANSPORT AND SCIENCE

The Greeks were greatly influenced by the Egyptians, particularly in science. The sciences then included religion, the arts, philosophy, astronomy, astrology and mathematics. It is in these areas that the ancient Greeks still affect modern thought today. Perhaps the strongest area of influence, after the arts, has been in philosophy. The Greek philosophers were imaginative, as were the mathematicians, who developed theories about atomic principles before they knew that atoms actually existed. Astronomers also introduced new theories. As long ago as the 6th century BCE, Anaxagoras discovered the moon did not give out light, but only reflected the light of the sun.

ROAD TO NOWHERE

Most Greek towns had good road systems. These were built with drainage channels and pavements. Some of the earliest examples of roads can be found in Crete. The example shown here is the Lechaion Road in Corinth. On mainland Greece, there were a few long-distance roads, but hardly any linking up the towns. The mountains made road-building very difficult.

MARITIME POWER

Because of its lack of natural resources, Greece depended on trade. Most of the major cities were located on islands scattered across the Aegean. The control of the trade routes by sea was vital to the empire.

PLATO

One of the most important Greek philosophers was Plato (c.427–347 BCE). He wrote several books discussing the origins of the universe and the relationship between man and the natural world. He lived in Athens and set up a school for philosophers.

SEAWORTHY

Around 1600 BCE, the Minoan civilization on the island of Crete improved ship design, making long sea voyages possible. The ships were powered by the combined use of oars (using slaves) and sails. A large oar at the stern acted as a rudder to steer the ship.

PYTHAGORAS

To the ancient Greeks, science and religion went together and so did an understanding of art and philosophy. Pythagoras (c.580–500 BCE) was born on the island of Samos and spent his life studying mathematics. Amongst his theories was the idea that all things were caused by numbers and mathematical relationships. He developed many mathematical principles, especially in geometry, which are still in use today.

TIME-HONOURED TRADITION

This modern photograph shows a peasant woman on Crete leading a donkey along a pack trail. Ancient Greeks would have done this, too. Beasts of burden, such as the donkey, were vital for transport where communities in the mountains could only be reached along narrow tracks.

PAN

Pan was one of the minor gods. The son of Hermes, he was half-man, half-goat, and the god of shepherds and flocks. He invented the pan-pipes and loved to spend time in the forest, hunting and dancing.

KING OF THE GODS

Cronos, youngest son of Uranos (Heaven), is said to have revolted against his father and married his sister, Rhea. To prevent his own sons replacing him, he ate each of his children at birth. When Zeus was born, Rhea wanted to save her son, and gave Cronos a stone to swallow instead. When he came of age, Zeus moved to Mount Olympus, near Macedonia.

GODDESS ATHENA

Athena was the daughter of Zeus and Metis. She was the goddess of wisdom and warfare. She was often accompanied by an owl and controlled the arts, literature, learning and philosophy. She became the patron goddess of Athens.

TEMPLES OF THE GODS

Each of the various Greek gods had their own special qualities and were worshipped in their own temple. By pleasing the gods, making offerings or animal sacrifices, believers hoped to win their favour. Greek towns had many fine temples, each one splendidly decorated.

RELIGION

Greek religion was polytheistic, that is they believed in many gods, not just one. The Greeks invented a very complex mythology to explain both the creation of the universe and the origins of the various gods. They saw the world before creation as Chaos, from which sprang the Earth (Ge, or Gaia), who gave birth to the Heavens (Uranos) and the sea (Pontus). The gods were human-like beings who lived on Mount Olympus, and often interfered in the affairs of man. Greek religion did not have a moral code. People simply had to please the gods to get what they wanted from life.

THE FALL OF ICARUS

Daedalus, a mythical craftsman, killed his nephew, Talos, in a jealous rage, and fled Athens for Crete with his son Icarus. They were later imprisoned by King Minos. They escaped using wings, fastened to their shoulders with wax. Icarus flew too close to the sun, melting the wax, and he fell into the sea and drowned.

SON OF ZEUS

Heracles, perhaps the greatest of all heroes, was the son of Zeus by a human woman, Alcmene. Although Heracles never became a god himself, he often asked them for their help. He is most famous for his Twelve Labours. When he died he was carried by a cloud to Olympus, where he became immortal and lived with the gods.

GODDESS OF LOVE

The relief above shows Aphrodite, the goddess of love, desire and fertility. She owned a magic girdle, which, if given to a human, made the wearer incredibly beautiful and desirable.

GREEK INFLUENCE

THE RENAISSANCE

In 17th-century Europe, many architects rejected medieval ideals in building design. They looked to the grandeur and elegance of classical Greece as their source of inspiration, known as the Renaissance.

S umeria, India and Egypt had already flourished and gone into decline long before the founding of the first Greek city-state. However, the founding of Minoan Crete was the first early civilization in Europe. Because ancient Greece was made it meant they were often fiercely independent. If the Greeks had formed a united empire, they may well have established an even greater civilization. It reached its peak in the 5th century BCE, leaving behind a magnificent legacy of art and architecture, science, sports, medicine, philosophy, and a system of government, all of which still form the basis of society today.

THE OLYMPIC GAMES

The sporting ideals created by the Greeks at their great games (particularly the Olympics) live on today. They first developed the idea that it is more important to compete and gain honour for one's community than to win.

DEMOCRACY

The governments of the Western World today are founded on the basic principles of democracy, from the Greek words 'demos', meaning people, and 'krakos', meaning power. Democracy was first developed in Athens in the 5th century BCE to replace monarchy. The system was not universally supported, however, and not everyone was represented; women, for example, were excluded from voting.

THE ROMAN EMPIRE

The Romans greatly respected the Greeks, modelling their own civilization upon theirs. They especially admired the magnificent yet simple elegance of Greek architecture.

PROTECTING THE PAST

For centuries, the magnificent remains of classical Greece lay unprotected and uncared for, and locals used the buildings as convenient stone quarries. During the 18th and, more particularly, the 19th century, interest in the ancient world was revived and many sites were excavated. A great many statues and artefacts were rescued and placed in museums around the world.

THEATRE-GOING

Theatre-going was probably started by the ancient Greeks and has remained a popular form of entertainment since those times. Modern theatre design is still based on Greek models, with a curved auditorium and seats rising in tiers from front to back.

HERITAGE

Perhaps the ancient Greek's finest legacy is the wealth of art and architectural remains, which are a source of inspiration to us today. Sadly, many of these remains have been lost, buried beneath modern towns, or deliberately destroyed for the sake of their materials.

GLOSSARY

Amphitheatre An open-air theatre for watching plays and sports. Usually a circular or oval area of ground around which rows of seats are arranged on a steep slope.

Artefact An object made by a person, such as a vase or a tool. Typically an item of cultural or historical interest.

Civilized A stage of cultural development considered to be more advanced.

Corruption Dishonest behaviour by those in power and often involving bribery.

Democracy A government system that believes in the equality of all people. Power is held by elected representatives.

Monarchy A country which has a king or a queen.

Mythology A set of stories or beliefs about a particular person or situation.

Philosophy The use of reason in understanding such things as the nature of reality and existence.

Polytheistic The belief in or worship of more than one god.

Relief Piece of art that is carved, moulded or stamped, so it stands out from the surface.

Sanitation Conditions relating to public health. Especially the provision of clean drinking water and adequate sewage disposal.

Siege A military operation in which enemy forces surround a town or building, cutting off essential supplies. The aim is to take control of the town or building.

ACKNOWLEDGEMENTS

We would like to thank Graham Rich, Rosie Hankin and Elizabeth Wiggans for their assistance.
Copyright © 2008 *ticktock* Entertainment Ltd.
First published in Great Britain by *ticktock* Media Ltd., Unit 2, Orchard Business Centre, North Farm Road, Tunbridge Wells, Kent, TN2 3XF, UK.
All rights reserved. No part of this publication may be reproduced, stored in a retrieval system, or transmitted in any form or by any means electronic, mechanical, photocopying, recording or otherwise, without prior written permission of the copyright owner.
A CIP catalogue record for this book is available from the British Library.
ISBN 978 1 84696 665 1
Picture research by Image Select.
Printed in China.
9 8 7 6 5 4 3 2

The original Greek spellings have been used where applicable, rather than the sometimes more familiar anglicized spellings.

Picture Credits: t=top, b=bottom, c=centre, l=left, r=right, IFC=inside front cover, OBC=outside back cover, OFC=outside front cover

AKG (London); 3cb, 4bl, 5br, 6/7cb, 7r, 7tl, 9tr, 8/9c, 10/11c & OFC, 12bl, 13br, 13t, 12/13ct, 17bl, 18bl, 18/19c, 18tl, 19tr & OFC, 22/23ø & OBC, 22bl, 22br, 24bl, 25r, 26b, 26tl, 27tl, 28tr, 28bl, OBC. CFCL/Image Select; 2tl, 27br, 30bl, 30tl. Giraudon; 2b, 4tl, 4tr, 5tr, 10tl, 11r, 12/13cb, 14tl, 14/15ct, 16r, 21br, 21tr, 20/21cb, 29br. Image Select; IFC, 4/5c, 10bl & 32ct & OBC, 10c, 10/11cb, 20/21ct, 20l, 21c, 22tr, 23tr & OFC, 28/29cb, 29cb, 30tr, 31br, 31tr. Pix; OFC (main pic), 2/3c, 3c, 6tl, 6bl, 6r, 6/7cb, 7r, 8t, 9br, 14/15 (main pic), 15tr, 17br. Ann Ronan @ Image Select; 8c, 12tl, 16tl, 17tr, 17tl, 19br, 21cl, 22tl, 23br, 24tl, 24/25c & OBC, 25tr, 27c, 27tr, 28tl, 29tr. Spectrum Colour Library; 30/31c, 31bl. Telegraph Colour Library UK; 8bl.

Every effort has been made to trace the copyright holders and we apologize in advance for any unintentional omissions.
We would be pleased to insert the appropriate acknowledgement in any subsequent edition of this publication.

INDEX